Dawn Delights

Mastering Overnight Oats for a Healthier Morning

Contents

Introduction

Welcome to "Dawn Delights: Mastering Overnight Oats for a Healthier Morning," your comprehensive guide to the nutritious world of overnight oats. This book is more than a recipe collection; it's a passport to a healthier, more convenient breakfast lifestyle.

If you've ever found yourself skipping breakfast or settling for unhealthy options due to morning rush, this book is your solution. Overnight oats offer a nutritious, delicious, and ready-to-eat breakfast when you wake up.

The magic of overnight oats lies in their simplicity and versatility. With a few basic ingredients and a mason jar, you can create a myriad of flavors and textures that will revolutionize your breakfast routine.

This book will guide you through the process of making overnight oats, starting with the basics. We'll explore the different types of oats, the best soaking liquids, and the ideal ratios for a perfect creamy texture.

We'll then journey through a world of flavors, from the sweetness of fruits to the richness of chocolate, from the crunch of nuts to the smoothness of yogurt. Each recipe is a unique gastronomic adventure.

We'll also venture into the less-explored territory of savory overnight oats, introducing a new dimension of breakfast flavors. If you've never tried savory oats before, prepare for a delightful surprise.

For those with dietary restrictions, we've included a range of vegan and gluten-free recipes that don't compromise on taste or nutrition. Everyone deserves a delightful dawn.

The book concludes with tips and tricks to customize your oats, store them properly, and troubleshoot common issues. This book is about understanding the process and making it your own.

Overnight oats are more than a breakfast dish. They're a canvas for culinary creativity, a tool for healthier living, and a testament to the magic of simple ingredients.

So, why overnight oats? They save time, they're versatile, they're nutritious, and above all, they're delicious.

Whether you're a busy professional, a parent trying to feed a family, a student on a budget, or just someone who loves good food, "Dawn Delights" is for you.

This book is more than a guide; it's a movement towards healthier mornings, delicious meals, and a better understanding of the food we eat.

So, are you ready to join this oat-filled adventure? Are you ready to transform your mornings? Are you ready to discover the delights that await you at dawn?

If the answer is yes, then let's begin. Your journey into the wonderful world of overnight oats starts now. Welcome to "Dawn Delights: Mastering Overnight Oats for a Healthier Morning."

As you embark on this journey, remember that cooking is not just about following recipes. It's about experimenting, understanding ingredients, and creating something that nourishes both your body and soul.

And that's what overnight oats are all about. They are a testament to the beauty of simplicity, the power of nutrition, and the joy of waking up to a breakfast that's ready to eat.

But don't be fooled by their simplicity. Overnight oats are a culinary playground. They invite you to play with flavors, to experiment with textures, to create something uniquely yours.

And that's the beauty of this book. It's not just a guide; it's an invitation. An invitation to explore, to experiment, to delight in the act of creating something delicious.

So, as you turn the pages, as you try the recipes, remember to have fun. Remember thateach jar of overnight oats is a reflection of you - your tastes, your creativity, your health journey.

And remember that each morning, as you open your fridge and reach for your jar of overnight oats, you're not just grabbing a breakfast. You're embracing a lifestyle. A lifestyle that values health, convenience, and of course, taste.

So, whether you're an overnight oats veteran looking for new inspiration, or a newbie ready to dip your toes into the world of soaked oats, this book has something for you.

And who knows? As you master the art of overnight oats, you might just find that your mornings become a little brighter, your days a little healthier, and your meals a lot more delicious.

So, are you ready to dive in? Are you ready to transform your breakfast game? Are you ready to discover the delights that await you at dawn?

If the answer is yes, then let's get started. Because a world of creamy, tasty, and nutritious overnight oats awaits you.

Welcome to "Dawn Delights: Mastering Overnight Oats for a Healthier Morning." Welcome to better mornings. Welcome to delicious, nutritious, and exciting breakfasts. Welcome to a world where the night works its magic, transforming simple ingredients into a breakfast that's worth waking up for. Welcome to a journey of taste, health, and convenience. Welcome to the delightful world of overnight oats.

So, let's turn the page. Let's start this adventure. Let's create some Dawn Delights. Your journey to mastering overnight oats for a healthier morning begins now. Enjoy the ride!

Here's to healthier, happier, and tastier mornings with "Dawn Delights: Mastering Overnight Oats for a Healthier Morning". Let's get started!

The Basics

Welcome to the world of overnight oats, where simplicity meets nutrition and convenience. Before we dive into the delicious recipes that await you, let's start with the basics. Understanding the fundamental ingredients and steps in making overnight oats is key to mastering this breakfast staple.

The first and most important ingredient in overnight oats is, of course, the **oats**. But not all oats are created equal. The type of oats you choose can significantly affect the texture and nutritional value of your breakfast.

There are several types of oats available in the market, but for overnight oats, the best option is **old-fashioned rolled oats**. These oats are whole oat groats that have been steamed and rolled into flakes. They absorb liquid well and maintain a nice, chewy texture even after soaking overnight.

Steel-cut oats, on the other hand, are whole oat groats that have been chopped into pieces but not rolled. They have a nuttier flavor and a chewier texture than rolled oats, but they don't absorb liquid as well. If you prefer your oats with a bit more bite, you can use steel-cut oats, but be prepared for a firmer, less creamy texture.

Instant or quick oats are not recommended for overnight oats. These oats have been pre-cooked, dried, and then rolled. They absorb liquid very quickly and can become mushy when soaked overnight.

The second key ingredient in overnight oats is the liquid. This is what the oats will absorb to become soft and creamy. The most common choice is **milk**, but there are many other options to suit different dietary needs and flavor preferences.

Cow's milk provides a creamy texture and a slightly sweet flavor. If you prefer a dairy-free option, almond milk, soy milk, oat milk, or any other **plant-based milk** can be used. Each of these options will impart a slightly different flavor to your oats.

For a tangier, creamier texture, you can use **yogurt** in addition to or instead of milk. **Greek yogurt** is a great option because it's high in protein and gives your oats a rich, creamy texture.

The ratio of oats to liquid is crucial in achieving the right consistency. A good starting point is a **1:2 ratio** of oats to liquid. That means for every 1 cup of oats, you'll use 2 cups of liquid. If you like your oats thinner, you can add more liquid. If you prefer them thicker, use less.

The third key ingredient in overnight oats is the **sweetener**. This is optional and can be adjusted to taste. The most common sweeteners are **honey, maple syrup, and agave nectar**. You can also use a sugar substitute or skip the sweetener altogether if you prefer.

Now that we've covered the basic ingredients, let's talk about the process. Making overnight oats is as simple as combining the oats, liquid, and sweetener in a jar, stirring them together, and letting them soak overnight in the refrigerator.

The soaking time is important. Overnight oats need at least **6 hours** to absorb the liquid and become soft. However, they can be left in the fridge for up to **5 days**. This makes them a great option for meal prep. You can make a batch at the beginning of the week and have breakfast ready for several days.

When you're ready to eat your oats, give them a good stir. The oats may have settled at the bottom of the jar, and the sweetener may need to be mixed in.

At this point, your basic overnight oats are ready to eat. But the real fun begins when you start adding toppings and mix-ins. Fruits, nuts, seeds, spices, and even protein powder can be added to enhance the flavor and nutritional value of your oats.

Fresh fruits like berries, bananas, and peaches add a natural sweetness and a burst of flavor to your oats. Dried fruits like raisins, cranberries, and apricots also work well and can be added before soaking to soften them up.

Nuts and seeds not only add a delightful crunch to your oats but also provide healthy fats and protein. **Almonds, walnuts, chia seeds, and flaxseeds** are all excellent choices.

Spices like **cinnamon, nutmeg, and vanilla extract** can add warmth and depth to your oats. They can be added before soaking to infuse the oats with flavor.

If you're looking to boost the protein content of your oats, a scoop of **protein powder** can do the trick. Just be sure to add a bit more liquid to compensate for the added dry ingredient.

Now, you might be wondering, can overnight oats be heated? The answer is yes. While overnight oats are typically eaten cold, straight from the fridge, they can also be warmed up in the microwave or on the stovetop if you prefer a hot breakfast.

To heat your oats, transfer them to a microwave-safe bowl and heat in the microwave for 1-2 minutes, stirring halfway through. If using the stovetop, transfer the oats to a pot and heat over medium heat, stirring occasionally, until warmed through.

1.

One of the best things about overnight oats is their portability. They're perfect for those busy mornings when you don't have time to sit down for breakfast. Just grab your jar of oats from the fridge, throw in a spoon, and you're good to go.

And there you have it - the basics of overnight oats. Simple, isn't it? But don't let the simplicity fool you. With these basic principles, you can create a multitude of delicious and nutritious breakfasts.

As you move on to the recipes in this book, remember these basics. Remember the importance of choosing the right type of oats, the 1:2 ratio of oats to liquid, and the soaking time.

But also remember that these are just guidelines. One of the beautiful things about overnight oats is their flexibility. Don't be afraid to experiment with different types of milk, sweeteners, and mix-ins. Make these oats your own.

Overnight oats are more than just a breakfast dish. They're a lifestyle. A lifestyle that values health, convenience, and taste. And with this book, you're well on your way to embracing this lifestyle.So, are you ready to dive into the world of overnight oats? If the answer is yes, then let's get started. The world of overnight oats awaits you. And trust me, it's a world worth exploring.

Fruit-Infused Overnight Oats

This section is all about adding a burst of natural sweetness and a wealth of nutrients to your morning oats. From the tangy freshness of berries to the tropical allure of mangoes, fruits can transform your overnight oats into a bowl of morning delight. Not only do fruits add a delicious flavor, but they also pack a nutritional punch, providing essential vitamins, minerals, and fiber. Whether you're a fan of classic combinations or looking for something exotic, there's a fruit-infused overnight oats recipe here for you.

APPLE CINNAMON OVERNIGHT OATS

This recipe brings together the comforting flavours of apple and cinnamon. It's a delightful way to start your day.

INGREDIENTS

- 1/2 cup rolled oats
- 1/2 cup almond milk
- 1/2 apple, diced
- 1/2 teaspoon cinnamon
- 1 tablespoon honey

METHOD

- In a jar, mix rolled oats and almond milk.
- Add diced apple and cinnamon.
- Stir in honey.
- Cover the jar and place it in the refrigerator overnight.
- Stir before serving. Enjoy cold.

MANGO COCONUT OVERNIGHT OATS

Tropical flavors of mango and coconut make this oatmeal recipe a refreshing and nutritious breakfast.

INGREDIENTS

- 1/2 cup rolled oats
- 1/2 cup coconut milk
- 1/4 cup diced mango
- 1 tablespoon shredded coconut
- 1 tablespoon honey

METHOD

- Mix rolled oats with coconut milk in a jar.
- Add diced mango and shredded coconut.
- Stir in honey.
- Cover the jar and refrigerate overnight.
- Give it a good stir before serving. Enjoy cold.

BERRY BLAST OVERNIGHT OATS

This berry-packed overnight oats recipe is filled with antioxidants. A perfect nutritious breakfast that tastes great.

INGREDIENTS

- 1/2 cup rolled oats
- 1/2 cup almond milk
- 1/4 cup mixed berries
- 1 tablespoon chia seeds
- 1 tablespoon honey

METHOD

- Combine rolled oats and almond milk in a jar.

- Add mixed berries and chia seeds.

- Stir in honey.

- Cover the jar and leave it in the refrigerator overnight.

- Stir well before serving. Enjoy cold.

PEACHY KEEN OVERNIGHT OATS

The sweet and tangy notes of ripe peaches combine perfectly with hearty oats in this summer-inspired recipe.

INGREDIENTS

- 1/2 cup rolled oats
- 1/2 cup almond milk
- 1/2 peach, diced
- 1 tablespoon chia seeds
- 1 tablespoon honey

METHOD

- Combine rolled oats and almond milk in a jar.
- Add diced peach and chia seeds.
- Stir in honey.
- Cover and refrigerate overnight.
- Stir well before serving. Enjoy cold.

BANANA NUT OVERNIGHT OATS

The classic combination of bananas and nuts make this overnight oats recipe a hearty and filling breakfast option.

INGREDIENTS

- 1/2 cup rolled oats
- 1/2 cup almond milk
- 1/2 banana, sliced
- 1 tablespoon nut butter
- 1 tablespoon honey

METHOD

- Mix rolled oats and almond milk in a jar.
- Add sliced banana and nut butter.
- Stir in honey.
- Cover and refrigerate overnight.
- Stir before serving. Enjoy cold.

TROPICAL PINEAPPLE OVERNIGHT OATS

The vibrant taste of pineapple brings a tropical touch to your breakfast table with this refreshing overnight oats recipe.

INGREDIENTS

- 1/2 cup rolled oats
- 1/2 cup coconut milk
- 1/4 cup pineapple chunks
- 1 tablespoon shredded coconut
- 1 tablespoon honey

METHOD

- Combine rolled oats and coconut milk in a jar.
- Add pineapple chunks and shredded coconut.
- Stir in honey.
- Cover and refrigerate overnight.
- Stir before serving. Enjoy cold.

RASPBERRY VANILLA OVERNIGHT OATS

This recipe delivers a delightful mix of tart raspberries and sweet vanilla, making your morning oats far from ordinary.

INGREDIENTS

- 1/2 cup rolled oats
- 1/2 cup almond milk
- 1/4 cup raspberries
- 1/2 teaspoon vanilla extract
- 1 tablespoon honey

METHOD

- Mix rolled oats and almond milk in a jar.
- Add raspberries and vanilla extract.
- Stir in honey.
- Cover and refrigerate overnight.
- Stir before serving. Enjoy cold.

BLUEBERRY LEMON OVERNIGHT OATS

The bright and fresh flavors of blueberries and lemon elevate these overnight oats to a deliciously zesty breakfast.

INGREDIENTS

- 1/2 cup rolled oats
- 1/2 cup almond milk
- 1/4 cup blueberries
- 1 teaspoon lemon zest
- 1 tablespoon honey

METHOD

- Combine rolled oats and almond milk in a jar.
- Add blueberries and lemon zest.
- Stir in honey.
- Cover and refrigerate overnight.
- Stir before serving. Enjoy cold.

CHERRY ALMOND OVERNIGHT OATS

Cherries and almonds offer a pleasing contrast of tart and sweet in these easy-to-prepare overnight oats.

INGREDIENTS

- 1/2 cup rolled oats
- 1/2 cup almond milk
- 1/4 cup cherries, pitted and chopped
- 1 tablespoon sliced almonds
- 1 tablespoon honey

METHOD

- Mix rolled oats and almond milk in a jar.
- Add chopped cherries and sliced almonds.
- Stir in honey.
- Cover and refrigerate overnight.
- Stir well before serving. Enjoy cold.

POMEGRANATE OVERNIGHT OATS

The tangy-sweet taste of pomegranate seeds adds a pop of flavor and color to this deliciously wholesome breakfast.

INGREDIENTS

- 1/2 cup rolled oats
- 1/2 cup almond milk
- 1/4 cup pomegranate seeds
- 1 tablespoon chia seeds
- 1 tablespoon honey

METHOD

- Combine rolled oats and almond milk in a jar.
- Add pomegranate seeds and chia seeds.
- Stir in honey.
- Cover and refrigerate overnight.
- Give it a good stir before serving. Enjoy cold.

Protein Packed Overnight Oats

If you're looking to boost your protein intake, improve muscle recovery, or simply keep yourself fuller for longer, you're in the right place. This section is dedicated to recipes that not only taste fantastic but also pack a powerful protein punch. From Greek yogurt and chia seeds to protein powders and nut butters, we'll explore a variety of ingredients that can supercharge your oats with protein. So, get ready to power up your mornings with these protein-packed overnight oats recipes.

PEANUT BUTTER BANANA PROTEIN OVERNIGHT OATS

The combination of peanut butter and banana delivers a protein-packed and delicious start to your day.

INGREDIENTS

- 1/2 cup rolled oats
- 1/2 cup almond milk
- 1/2 banana, sliced
- 1 tablespoon peanut butter
- 1 scoop protein powder

METHOD

- Mix rolled oats, protein powder, and almond milk in a jar.
- Add sliced banana and peanut butter.
- Stir well to combine.
- Cover and refrigerate overnight.
- Stir well before serving. Enjoy cold.

CHOCOLATE ALMOND PROTEIN OVERNIGHT OATS

This recipe offers the satisfying combination of chocolate and almond, with the added benefit of protein.

INGREDIENTS

- 1/2 cup rolled oats
- 1/2 cup almond milk
- 1 tablespoon almond butter
- 1 tablespoon cocoa powder
- 1 scoop protein powder

METHOD

- Combine rolled oats, protein powder, cocoa powder, and almond milk in a jar.
- Add almond butter.
- Stir until well combined.
- Cover and refrigerate overnight.
- Stir before serving. Enjoy cold.

BLUEBERRY VANILLA PROTEIN OVERNIGHT OATS

Start your day with the delightful mix of blueberries and vanilla, plus a boost of protein in these overnight oats.

INGREDIENTS

- 1/2 cup rolled oats
- 1/2 cup almond milk
- 1/4 cup blueberries
- 1 scoop vanilla protein powder

METHOD

- Combine rolled oats, protein powder, cocoa powder, and almond milk in a jar.
- Add almond butter.
- Stir until well combined.
- Cover and refrigerate overnight.
- Stir before serving. Enjoy cold.

GREEK YOGURT STRAWBERRY PROTEIN OVERNIGHT OATS

This recipe mixes the tangy sweetness of strawberries with protein-rich Greek yogurt for a refreshing breakfast.

INGREDIENTS

- 1/2 cup rolled oats
- 1/2 cup Greek yogurt
- 1/4 cup almond milk
- 1/4 cup strawberries, sliced
- 1 scoop protein powder

METHOD

- Combine rolled oats, protein powder, Greek yogurt, and almond milk in a jar.
- Add sliced strawberries.
- Stir well to combine.
- Cover and refrigerate overnight.
- Stir well before serving. Enjoy cold.

CINNAMON ROLL PROTEIN OVERNIGHT OATS

Enjoy the flavors of a cinnamon roll in a healthy, protein-packed overnight oats recipe.

INGREDIENTS

- 1/2 cup rolled oats
- 1/2 cup almond milk
- 1 tablespoon cinnamon
- 1 tablespoon honey
- 1 scoop vanilla protein powder

METHOD

- Mix rolled oats, protein powder, cinnamon, and almond milk in a jar.
- Stir in honey.
- Cover and refrigerate overnight.
- Stir well before serving. Enjoy cold.

MOCHA PROTEIN OVERNIGHT OATS

For the coffee lovers out there, this mocha-infused protein-packed overnight oats recipe is a perfect breakfast treat.

INGREDIENTS

- 1/2 cup rolled oats
- 1/2 cup brewed coffee
- 1 tablespoon cocoa powder
- 1 tablespoon honey
- 1 scoop protein powder

METHOD

- Combine rolled oats, protein powder, cocoa powder, and brewed coffee in a jar.
- Stir in honey.
- Cover and refrigerate overnight.
- Stir well before serving. Enjoy cold.

COCONUT CHIA PROTEIN OVERNIGHT OATS

This recipe brings the tropical flavor of coconut and the crunch of chia seeds to your protein-packed oats.

INGREDIENTS

- 1/2 cup rolled oats
- 1/2 cup coconut milk
- 1 tablespoon chia seeds
- 1 tablespoon honey
- 1 scoop protein powder

METHOD

- Mix rolled oats, protein powder, chia seeds, and coconut milk in a jar.
- Stir in honey.
- Cover and refrigerate overnight.
- Stir well before serving. Enjoy cold.

MAPLE PECAN PROTEIN OVERNIGHT OATS

The classic flavors of maple and pecan blend perfectly in this protein-rich overnight oats recipe.

INGREDIENTS

- 1/2 cup rolled oats
- 1/2 cup almond milk
- 1 tablespoon pecans, chopped
- 1 tablespoon maple syrup
- 1 scoop protein powder

METHOD

- Combine rolled oats, protein powder, pecans, and almond milk in a jar.
- Stir in maple syrup.
- Cover and refrigerate overnight.
- Stir well before serving. Enjoy cold.

APPLE PIE PROTEIN OVERNIGHT OATS

Enjoy the comforting flavors of apple pie in a hearty, protein-packed overnight oats recipe.

INGREDIENTS

- 1/2 cup rolled oats
- 1/2 cup almond milk
- 1/2 apple, chopped
- 1 teaspoon cinnamon
- 1 tablespoon honey
- 1 scoop protein powder

METHOD

- Combine rolled oats, protein powder, cinnamon, and almond milk in a jar.
- Add chopped apple.
- Stir in honey.
- Cover and refrigerate overnight.
- Stir well before serving. Enjoy cold.

PUMPKIN SPICE PROTEIN OVERNIGHT OATS

The warm flavors of pumpkin spice make these protein-rich overnight oats a delightful autumn-inspired breakfast.

INGREDIENTS

- /2 cup rolled oats
- 1/2 cup almond milk
- 1/4 cup pumpkin puree
- 1 teaspoon pumpkin spice
- 1 tablespoon maple syrup
- 1 scoop protein powder

METHOD

- Mix rolled oats, protein powder, pumpkin spice, and almond milk in a jar.
- Add pumpkin puree.
- Stir in maple syrup.
- Cover and refrigerate overnight.
- Stir well before serving. Enjoy cold.

Sweet Treat Overnight Oats

If you've got a sweet tooth, this section is your paradise. Here, we'll explore how to transform your overnight oats into indulgent yet healthy treats that will make your mornings feel like a celebration. From the rich decadence of chocolate to the natural sweetness of honey and fruits, these recipes are designed to satisfy your cravings without compromising on nutrition. So, get ready to start your day on a sweet note with these irresistible overnight oats recipes.

CHOCOLATE PEANUT BUTTER OVERNIGHT OATS

This combines the classic and irresistible combo of chocolate and peanut butter to start your day with a sweet treat.

INGREDIENTS

- 1/2 cup rolled oats
- 1/2 cup almond milk
- 1 tablespoon cocoa powder
- 1 tablespoon peanut butter
- 1 tablespoon honey

METHOD

- Combine rolled oats and almond milk in a jar.
- Add cocoa powder and peanut butter.
- Stir in honey.
- Cover and refrigerate overnight.
- Stir well before serving. Enjoy cold.

COCONUT CREAM PIE OVERNIGHT OATS

Get a taste of dessert for breakfast with these creamy and coconut-flavored overnight oats.

INGREDIENTS

- 1/2 cup rolled oats
- 1/2 cup coconut milk
- 1 tablespoon shredded coconut
- 1 tablespoon honey

METHOD

- Mix rolled oats and coconut milk in a jar.
- Add shredded coconut.
- Stir in honey.
- Cover and refrigerate overnight.
- Stir before serving. Enjoy cold.

PUMPKIN SPICE DELUX OVERNIGHT OATS

Get a taste of dessert for breakfast with these creamy and coconut-flavored overnight oats.

INGREDIENTS

- 1/2 cup rolled oats
- 1/2 cup almond milk
- 1/4 cup pumpkin puree
- 1/2 teaspoon pumpkin spice
- 1 tablespoon honey
- Handful raisins

METHOD

- Combine rolled oats and almond milk in a jar.
- Add pumpkin puree, raisins and pumpkin spice.
- Stir in honey.
- Cover and refrigerate overnight.
- Stir before serving. Enjoy cold.

LEMON POPPY SEED OVERNIGHT OATS

With a burst of lemon flavor and a crunch of poppy seeds, these overnight oats are a refreshing way to start your day.

INGREDIENTS

- 1/2 cup rolled oats
- 1/2 cup almond milk
- 1 tablespoon lemon juice
- 1 teaspoon lemon zest
- 1 tablespoon poppy seeds
- 1 tablespoon honey

METHOD

- Mix rolled oats and almond milk in a jar.

- Add lemon juice, lemon zest, and poppy seeds.

- Stir in honey.

- Cover and refrigerate overnight.

- Stir well before serving. Enjoy cold.

CARAMEL APPLE OVERNIGHT OATS

This recipe brings the classic flavors of a caramel apple into a wholesome and hearty breakfast.

INGREDIENTS

- 1/2 cup rolled oats
- 1/2 cup almond milk
- 1/2 apple, diced
- 1 tablespoon caramel sauce
- 1 tablespoon honey

METHOD

- Combine rolled oats and almond milk in a jar.

- Add diced apple and caramel sauce.

- Stir in honey.

- Cover and refrigerate overnight.

- Stir before serving. Enjoy cold.

STRAWBERRY CHEESECAKE OVERNIGHT OATS

This recipe brings the delightful flavors of a strawberry cheesecake to your breakfast table, sans the guilt.

INGREDIENTS

- 1/2 cup rolled oats
- 1/2 cup almond milk
- 1/4 cup diced strawberries
- 1 tablespoon cream cheese
- 1 tablespoon honey

METHOD

- Combine rolled oats and almond milk in a jar.
- Add diced strawberries and cream cheese.
- Stir in honey.
- Cover and refrigerate overnight.
- Stir well before serving. Enjoy cold.

ALMOND JOY OVERNIGHT OATS

This recipe brings the delightful flavors of a strawberry cheesecake to your breakfast table, sans the guilt.

INGREDIENTS

- 1/2 cup rolled oats
- 1/2 cup almond milk
- 1 tablespoon cocoa powder
- 1 tablespoon shredded coconut
- 1 tablespoon sliced almonds
- 1 tablespoon honey

METHOD

- Mix rolled oats and almond milk in a jar.

- Add cocoa powder, shredded coconut, and sliced almonds.

- Stir in honey.

- Cover and refrigerate overnight.

- Stir before serving. Enjoy cold.

BLUEBERRY MUFFIN OVERNIGHT OATS

Get the taste of a blueberry muffin in a healthier, easy-to-make format with these overnight oats.

INGREDIENTS

- 1/2 cup rolled oats
- 1/2 cup almond milk
- 1/4 cup blueberries
- 1/2 teaspoon vanilla extract
- 1 tablespoon honey

METHOD

- Combine rolled oats and almond milk in a jar.
- Add blueberries and vanilla extract.
- Stir in honey.
- Cover and refrigerate overnight.
- Stir before serving. Enjoy cold.

MAPLE BROWN SUGAR OVERNIGHT OATS

This recipe brings the comforting flavors of maple and brown sugar to your morning oats.

INGREDIENTS

- 1/2 cup rolled oats
- 1/2 cup almond milk
- 1 tablespoon maple syrup
- 1 tablespoon brown sugar

METHOD

- Mix rolled oats and almond milk in a jar.
- Stir in maple syrup and brown sugar.
- Cover and refrigerate overnight.
- Stir well before serving. Enjoy cold.

RASPBERRY WHITE CHOCOLATE OVERNIGHT OATS

Sweet and tart raspberries pair perfectly with creamy white chocolate in these indulgent overnight oats.

INGREDIENTS

- 1/2 cup rolled oats
- 1/2 cup almond milk
- 1/4 cup raspberries
- 1 tablespoon white chocolate chips
- 1 tablespoon honey

METHOD

- Combine rolled oats and almond milk in a jar.
- Add raspberries and white chocolate chips.
- Stir in honey.
- Cover and refrigerate overnight.
- Stir before serving. Enjoy cold.

Savory Overnight Oats

Welcome to the exciting world of Savory Overnight Oats! If you thought oats were only for sweet breakfasts, prepare to have your culinary horizons expanded. This section is dedicated to those who crave a hearty, savory start to their day. We're about to explore a variety of recipes that incorporate vegetables, cheeses, herbs, and even proteins into our beloved overnight oats. These recipes will challenge your perception of oats and introduce you to a whole new realm of flavors.

ITALIAN HERB AND TOMATO OVERNIGHT OATS

This recipe brings a savory spin to overnight oats, with robust Italian herbs and juicy tomatoes.

INGREDIENTS

- 1/2 cup rolled oats
- 1/2 cup vegetable broth
- 1/4 cup chopped tomatoes
- 1 tablespoon Italian herbs
- Salt and pepper to taste

METHOD

- Combine oats and vegetable broth in a jar.
- Add chopped tomatoes and herbs.
- Season with salt and pepper.
- Cover and refrigerate overnight.
- Stir well before serving. Enjoy cold or heated up.

GARLIC MUSHROOM OVERNIGHT OATS

The earthy flavors of mushroom and garlic come together in this hearty and satisfying recipe.

INGREDIENTS

- 1/2 cup rolled oats
- 1/2 cup vegetable broth
- 1/4 cup sliced mushrooms
- 1 clove garlic, minced
- Salt and pepper to taste

METHOD

- Mix oats and vegetable broth in a jar.
- Add sliced mushrooms and minced garlic.
- Season with salt and pepper.
- Cover and refrigerate overnight.
- Stir before serving. Enjoy cold or heated up.

ZESTY LEMON AND DILL OVERNIGHT OATS

The bright, fresh flavors of lemon and dill lighten up these savory oats, making it a perfect summer breakfast.

INGREDIENTS

- 1/2 cup rolled oats
- 1/2 cup vegetable broth
- 1 tablespoon lemon juice
- 1 tablespoon fresh dill, chopped
- Salt and pepper to taste

METHOD

- Combine oats and vegetable broth in a jar.
- Add lemon juice and chopped dill.
- Season with salt and pepper.
- Cover and refrigerate overnight.
- Stir before serving. Enjoy cold or heated up.

SPICED CURRY OVERNIGHT OATS

This recipe brings a kick of Indian flavors to your morning oats, featuring a warming curry spice blend.

INGREDIENTS

- 1/2 cup rolled oats
- 1/2 cup coconut milk
- 1 teaspoon curry powder
- Salt to taste

METHOD

- Mix oats and coconut milk in a jar.
- Stir in curry powder and salt.
- Cover and refrigerate overnight.
- Stir before serving. Enjoy cold or heated up.

SALSA AND AVOCADO OVERNIGHT OATS

This recipe brings a Mexican twist to your oats, with tangy salsa and creamy avocado.

INGREDIENTS

- 1/2 cup rolled oats
- 1/2 cup vegetable broth
- 1/4 cup salsa
- 1/4 avocado, diced
- Salt to taste

METHOD

- Combine oats and vegetable broth in a jar.

- Add salsa and diced avocado.

- Season with salt.

- Cover and refrigerate overnight.

- Stir well before serving. Enjoy cold or heated up.

MEDITERRANEAN FETA AND OLIVE OVERNIGHT OATS

Enjoy the flavors of the Mediterranean with tangy feta and briny olives in this savory overnight oats recipe.

INGREDIENTS

- 1/2 cup rolled oats
- 1/2 cup vegetable broth
- 1/4 cup crumbled feta cheese
- 1 tablespoon chopped olives
- Salt and pepper to taste

METHOD

- Mix oats and vegetable broth in a jar.
- Add feta cheese and chopped olives.
- Season with salt and pepper.
- Cover and refrigerate overnight.
- Stir before serving. Enjoy cold or heated up.

ASIAN-INSPIRED SOY AND SESAME OVERNIGHT OATS

This recipe infuses your morning oats with savory Asian flavors, featuring soy sauce and sesame seeds.

INGREDIENTS

- 1/2 cup rolled oats
- 1/2 cup vegetable broth
- 1 teaspoon soy sauce
- 1 teaspoon sesame seeds
- Green onions, chopped for garnish

METHOD

- Combine oats and vegetable broth in a jar.
- Add soy sauce and sesame seeds.
- Cover and refrigerate overnight.
- Before serving, stir and top with chopped green onions.
- Enjoy cold or heated up.

HERBED GOAT CHEESE AND TOMATO OVERNIGHT OATS

Enjoy a French-inspired breakfast with herbed goat cheese and fresh tomatoes in these savory oats.

INGREDIENTS

- 1/2 cup rolled oats
- 1/2 cup vegetable broth
- 1/4 cup herbed goat cheese
- 1/4 cup chopped tomatoes
- Salt and pepper to taste

METHOD

- Mix oats and vegetable broth in a jar.
- Add herbed goat cheese and chopped tomatoes.
- Season with salt and pepper.
- Cover and refrigerate overnight.
- Stir before serving. Enjoy cold or heated up.

PESTO AND PARMESAN OVERNIGHT OATS

Italian-inspired overnight oats featuring flavorful pesto and rich Parmesan cheese make for a delectable savory breakfast.

INGREDIENTS

- 1/2 cup rolled oats
- 1/2 cup vegetable broth
- 1 tablespoon pesto
- 2 tablespoons grated Parmesan cheese
- Salt to taste

METHOD

- Combine oats and vegetable broth in a jar.

- Add pesto and grated Parmesan cheese.

- Season with salt.

- Cover and refrigerate overnight.

- Stir before serving. Enjoy cold or heated up.

SUN-DRIED TOMATO AND SPINACH OVERNIGHT OATS

This recipe brings the rich flavor of sun-dried tomatoes with fresh spinach for a nutrient-packed start to your day.

INGREDIENTS

- 1/2 cup rolled oats
- 1/2 cup vegetable broth
- 1/4 cup sun-dried tomatoes, chopped
- 1/4 cup fresh spinach, chopped
- Salt and pepper to taste

METHOD

- Mix oats and vegetable broth in a jar.
- Add sun-dried tomatoes and chopped spinach.
- Season with salt and pepper.
- Cover and refrigerate overnight.
- Stir before serving. Enjoy cold or heated up.

Vegan and Gluten-Free Overnight Oats

Here, we'll delve into the world of plant-based milks, gluten-free oats, and a variety of flavorful, nutritious ingredients that align with vegan and gluten-free diets. We'll showcase how dietary restrictions don't limit your options, but rather open up a new realm of delicious possibilities.

VEGAN APPLE CINNAMON OVERNIGHT OATS

A vegan twist on a classic, these apple cinnamon overnight oats are a comforting and wholesome breakfast option.

INGREDIENTS

- 1/2 cup gluten-free rolled oats
- 1/2 cup almond milk
- 1/2 apple, diced
- 1/2 teaspoon cinnamon
- 1 tablespoon maple syrup

METHOD

- Combine rolled oats and almond milk in a jar.
- Add diced apple and cinnamon.
- Stir in maple syrup.
- Cover and refrigerate overnight.
- Stir well before serving. Enjoy cold.

VEGAN BERRY BLISS OVERNIGHT OATS

Packed with antioxidants from a medley of berries, these vegan overnight oats are as nutritious as they are delicious.

INGREDIENTS

- 1/2 cup gluten-free rolled oats
- 1/2 cup almond milk
- 1/4 cup mixed berries
- 1 tablespoon chia seeds
- 1 tablespoon maple syrup

METHOD

- Mix rolled oats and almond milk in a jar.

- Add mixed berries and chia seeds.

- Stir in maple syrup.

- Cover and refrigerate overnight.

- Stir before serving. Enjoy cold.

VEGAN CHOCOLATE BANANA OVERNIGHT OATS

Who says you can't have chocolate for breakfast? These vegan chocolate banana overnight oats are a treat to wake up to.

INGREDIENTS

- 1/2 cup gluten-free rolled oats
- 1/2 cup almond milk
- 1/2 banana, sliced
- 1 tablespoon cocoa powder
- 1 tablespoon maple syrup

METHOD

- Combine rolled oats and almond milk in a jar.
- Add sliced banana and cocoa powder.
- Stir in maple syrup.
- Cover and refrigerate overnight.
- Stir well before serving. Enjoy cold.

VEGAN TROPICAL OVERNIGHT OATS

Bring a tropical twist to your breakfast with these refreshing overnight oats, featuring the flavors of pineapple and coconut.

INGREDIENTS

- 1/2 cup gluten-free rolled oats
- 1/2 cup coconut milk
- 1/4 cup diced pineapple
- 1 tablespoon shredded coconut
- 1 tablespoon agave nectar

METHOD

- Mix rolled oats and coconut milk in a jar.
- Add diced pineapple and shredded coconut.
- Stir in agave nectar.
- Cover and refrigerate overnight.
- Stir before serving. Enjoy cold.

VEGAN STRAWBERRY KIWI OVERNIGHT OATS

Bright and fresh, these strawberry kiwi overnight oats are a sweet way to start your day.

INGREDIENTS

- 1/2 cup gluten-free rolled oats
- 1/2 cup almond milk
- 1/4 cup diced strawberries
- 1/4 cup diced kiwi
- 1 tablespoon chia seeds
- 1 tablespoon agave nectar

METHOD

- Combine rolled oats and almond milk in a jar.
- Add diced strawberries, kiwi, and chia seeds.
- Stir in agave nectar.
- Cover and refrigerate overnight.
- Stir before serving. Enjoy cold.

VEGAN GINGER PEACH OVERNIGHT OATS

The warming spice of ginger pairs beautifully with sweet peaches in this flavor-packed overnight oats recipe.

INGREDIENTS

- 1/2 cup gluten-free rolled oats
- 1/2 cup almond milk
- 1/2 peach, diced
- 1/2 teaspoon ginger, grated
- 1 tablespoon maple syrup

METHOD

- Mix rolled oats and almond milk in a jar.
- Add diced peach and grated ginger.
- Stir in maple syrup.
- Cover and refrigerate overnight.
- Stir well before serving. Enjoy cold.

VEGAN BLUEBERRY LEMON OVERNIGHT OATS

The zesty brightness of lemon and the sweet notes of blueberries make a delightful contrast in these overnight oats.

INGREDIENTS

- 1/2 cup gluten-free rolled oats
- 1/2 cup almond milk
- 1/4 cup blueberries
- 1 teaspoon lemon zest
- 1 tablespoon agave nectar

METHOD

- Combine rolled oats and almond milk in a jar.
- Add blueberries and lemon zest.
- Stir in agave nectar.
- Cover and refrigerate overnight.
- Stir well before serving. Enjoy cold.

VEGAN MATCHA RASPBERRY OVERNIGHT OATS

Get a boost of antioxidants with these matcha raspberry overnight oats. A healthy and delicious start to your day.

INGREDIENTS

- 1/2 cup gluten-free rolled oats
- 1/2 cup almond milk
- 1/4 cup raspberries
- 1 teaspoon matcha powder
- 1 tablespoon maple syrup

METHOD

- Mix rolled oats and almond milk in a jar.
- Add raspberries and matcha powder.
- Stir in maple syrup.
- Cover and refrigerate overnight.
- Stir before serving. Enjoy cold.

VEGAN POMEGRANATE OVERNIGHT OATS

These pomegranate overnight oats not only taste great, they pack in a good dose of antioxidants for a nutritious breakfast.

INGREDIENTS

- 1/2 cup gluten-free rolled oats
- 1/2 cup almond milk
- 1/4 cup pomegranate seeds
- 1 tablespoon chia seeds
- 1 tablespoon agave nectar

METHOD

- Combine rolled oats and almond milk in a jar.
- Add pomegranate seeds and chia seeds.
- Stir in agave nectar.
- Cover and refrigerate overnight.
- Stir well before serving. Enjoy cold.

VEGAN CHIA ALMOND OVERNIGHT OATS

These overnight oats feature the satisfying crunch of almonds and the healthful benefits of chia seeds for a filling breakfast.

INGREDIENTS

- 1/2 cup gluten-free rolled oats
- 1/2 cup almond milk
- 1 tablespoon chia seeds
- 1 tablespoon chopped almonds
- 1 tablespoon maple syrup

METHOD

- Mix rolled oats and almond milk in a jar.
- Add chia seeds and chopped almonds.
- Stir in maple syrup.
- Cover and refrigerate overnight.
- Stir well before serving. Enjoy cold.

Seasonal Overnight Oats

From the fresh berries of summer to the hearty spices of winter, each season brings its unique produce and flavors. And what better way to enjoy them than in a nourishing jar of overnight oats?

In this section, we'll explore a variety of recipes that highlight the best of each season's offerings. Whether it's a refreshing spring-inspired oats jar brimming with citrus fruits or a cozy autumnal oats bowl with pumpkin and cinnamon, there's a recipe for every season and every palate.

WINTER WONDERLAND OVERNIGHT OATS

This recipe captures the essence of winter with its use of warm spices and wintery fruits like oranges and dates.

INGREDIENTS

- 1/2 cup rolled oats
- 1/2 cup almond milk
- 1/4 cup diced dates
- 1/2 orange, zest and juice
- 1/4 teaspoon cinnamon
- 1 tablespoon honey

METHOD

- In a jar, mix rolled oats with almond milk.
- Add diced dates, orange zest, and juice.
- Sprinkle cinnamon and stir in honey.
- Cover and refrigerate overnight.
- Stir before serving. Enjoy cold.

SPRING AWAKENING OVERNIGHT OATS

Celebrate spring with this bright, refreshing overnight oats recipe that highlights strawberries and lemon.

INGREDIENTS

- 1/2 cup rolled oats
- 1/2 cup almond milk
- 1/4 cup diced strawberries
- 1/2 lemon, zest and juice
- 1 tablespoon chia seeds
- 1 tablespoon honey

METHOD

- Combine rolled oats and almond milk in a jar.

- Add diced strawberries, lemon zest, and juice.

- Sprinkle chia seeds and stir in honey.

- Cover and refrigerate overnight.

- Stir before serving. Enjoy cold.

SUMMER BURST OVERNIGHT OATS

Embrace the taste of summer with this tropical-inspired overnight oats recipe featuring pineapple and coconut.

INGREDIENTS

- 1/2 cup rolled oats
- 1/2 cup coconut milk
- 1/4 cup diced pineapple
- 1 tablespoon shredded coconut
- 1 tablespoon chia seeds
- 1 tablespoon honey

METHOD

- Mix rolled oats with coconut milk in a jar.

- Add diced pineapple and shredded coconut.

- Sprinkle chia seeds and stir in honey.

- Cover and refrigerate overnight.

- Stir before serving. Enjoy cold.

AUTUMN HARVEST OVERNIGHT OATS

This recipe captures the flavors of fall with its use of warming spices and fall fruits like apples and cranberries.

INGREDIENTS

- 1/2 cup rolled oats
- 1/2 cup almond milk
- 1/2 apple, diced
- 1/4 cup dried cranberries
- 1/4 teaspoon cinnamon
- 1 tablespoon maple syrup

METHOD

- In a jar, mix rolled oats with almond milk.
- Add diced apple and dried cranberries.
- Sprinkle cinnamon and stir in maple syrup.
- Cover and refrigerate overnight.
- Stir before serving. Enjoy cold.

EARLY SPRING MATCHA OVERNIGHT OATS

Welcome the arrival of spring with this invigorating overnight oats recipe featuring the unique flavor of matcha green tea.

INGREDIENTS

- 1/2 cup rolled oats
- 1/2 cup almond milk
- 1 teaspoon matcha powder
- 1 banana, sliced
- 1 tablespoon chia seeds
- 1 tablespoon honey

METHOD

- Mix rolled oats and almond milk in a jar.
- Stir in matcha powder until well combined.
- Add sliced banana and chia seeds.
- Stir in honey.
- Cover and refrigerate overnight.
- Stir before serving. Enjoy cold.

SUMMER BERRY BLAST OVERNIGHT OATS

The vibrant, sweet flavors of summer berries make this overnight oats recipe a refreshing breakfast on summer days.

INGREDIENTS

- 1/2 cup rolled oats
- 1/2 cup almond milk
- 1/4 cup mixed berries (raspberries, blueberries, blackberries)
- 1 tablespoon chia seeds
- 1 tablespoon honey

METHOD

- Combine rolled oats and almond milk in a jar.
- Add mixed berries and chia seeds.
- Stir in honey.
- Cover and refrigerate overnight.
- Stir before serving. Enjoy cold.

WINTER CITRUS OVERNIGHT OATS

Brighten up cold winter mornings with this refreshing overnight oats recipe featuring fresh citrus fruits.

INGREDIENTS

- 1/2 cup rolled oats
- 1/2 cup almond milk
- 1/4 cup fresh orange segments
- 1/2 grapefruit, segments
- 1 tablespoon chia seeds
- 1 tablespoon honey

METHOD

- Combine rolled oats and almond milk in a jar.

- Add orange and grapefruit segments.

- Sprinkle chia seeds and stir in honey.

- Cover and refrigerate overnight.

- Stir before serving. Enjoy cold.

SPRINGTIME HONEY ALMOND OVERNIGHT OATS

Honey and almond bring a taste of the blossoming spring to your breakfast with this easy overnight oats recipe.

INGREDIENTS

- 1/2 cup rolled oats
- 1/2 cup almond milk
- 1 tablespoon almond butter
- 1 tablespoon honey
- 1 tablespoon sliced almonds
- A pinch of salt

METHOD

- Mix rolled oats and almond milk in a jar.
- Stir in almond butter and honey.
- Sprinkle sliced almonds and a pinch of salt.
- Cover and refrigerate overnight.
- Stir well before serving. Enjoy cold.

SUMMER SUNSHINE OVERNIGHT OATS

Enjoy a taste of summer with this sunny overnight oats recipe featuring mango and coconut, a tropical delight!

INGREDIENTS

- 1/2 cup rolled oats
- 1/2 cup coconut milk
- 1/4 cup mango chunks
- 1 tablespoon shredded coconut
- 1 tablespoon honey

METHOD

- In a jar, mix rolled oats with coconut milk.
- Add mango chunks and shredded coconut.
- Drizzle in honey.
- Cover and refrigerate overnight.
- Stir well before serving. Enjoy cold.

AUTUMN APPLE CINNAMON OVERNIGHT OATS

Cozy up with the warming flavors of fall with these apple cinnamon overnight oats, like having apple pie for breakfast!

INGREDIENTS

- 1/2 cup rolled oats
- 1/2 cup almond milk
- 1/2 apple, diced
- 1/4 teaspoon ground cinnamon
- 1 tablespoon chia seeds
- 1 tablespoon maple syrup

METHOD

- Combine rolled oats and almond milk in a jar.

- Add diced apple and ground cinnamon.

- Sprinkle chia seeds and stir in maple syrup.

- Cover and refrigerate overnight.

- Give it a good stir before serving. Enjoy cold.

Tips and Tricks for Perfect Overnight Oats

As we reach the end of our journey through the world of overnight oats, it's time to share some final tips and tricks. These nuggets of wisdom will help you perfect your overnight oats and make your breakfast experience even more delightful.

First, let's talk about the oats. Remember, the type of oats you choose can significantly affect the texture of your overnight oats. Old-fashioned rolled oats are the best choice for a creamy, chewy texture. Steel-cut oats can be used for a heartier, chewier texture, but they may not soften as much as rolled oats.

When it comes to the liquid, feel free to experiment. Different types of milk will give your oats different flavors. Cow's milk will make your oats creamy and slightly sweet, while almond milk will give them a nutty flavor. Don't be afraid to try different types of milk to find your favorite.

The sweetness of your oats can also be adjusted to your liking. If you prefer your oats less sweet, you can reduce the amount of sweetener or even skip it altogether. Remember, you can always add more sweetness in the morning if needed.

The soaking time is crucial for achieving the perfect texture. Overnight oats should be soaked for at least 6 hours, but not more than 5 days. If you soak your oats for too long, they may become too soft and lose their chewy texture.

When it comes to toppings and mix-ins, the sky's the limit. Fruits, nuts, seeds, spices, and even protein powder can be added to your oats for extra flavor and nutrition. But remember, less is often more. Don't overload your oats with too many toppings, or you might overwhelm the flavors.

If you're adding fresh fruits or nuts to your oats, it's best to add them in the morning before eating. This will keep the fruits fresh and the nuts crunchy. If you're using dried fruits or seeds, you can add them the night before to let them soften.

If you prefer your oats warm, you can heat them up in the microwave or on the stovetop. Just remember to transfer your oats to a microwave-safe bowl or a pot before heating.

Overnight oats are perfect for meal prep. You can make a batch at the beginning of the week and have breakfast ready for several days. Just remember to store your oats in the fridge, and they should stay fresh for up to 5 days.

Finally, remember that making overnight oats is not an exact science. It's a creative process that allows you to experiment with different flavors and textures. Don't be afraid to try new things and make the recipes your own.

And there you have it – your guide to perfect overnight oats. With these tips and tricks, you're well on your way to mastering the art of overnight oats.

As we conclude this book, I hope you feel inspired and equipped to start your own overnight oats journey. Remember, overnight oats are more than just a breakfast dish. They're a lifestyle. A lifestyle that values health, convenience, and taste.

So, as you embark on your overnight oats adventure, remember to have fun. Remember to experiment. Remember to savor each bite. Because that's what overnight oats are all about.

Thank you for joining me on this journey. I hope you've enjoyed it as much as I have. I hope you've learned something new. But most importantly, I hope you've discovered the delights that await you at dawn.

Printed in Great Britain
by Amazon